BEYOND THE GREAT MOUNTAINS

A VISUAL POEM ABOUT CHINA

chronicle books · san francisco

MOUNTAIN
PEAKS

BEYOND THE GREAT MOUNTAINS,

EAST

TREE

SUN

FAR TO THE EAST, A VAST FERTILE PLAIN.

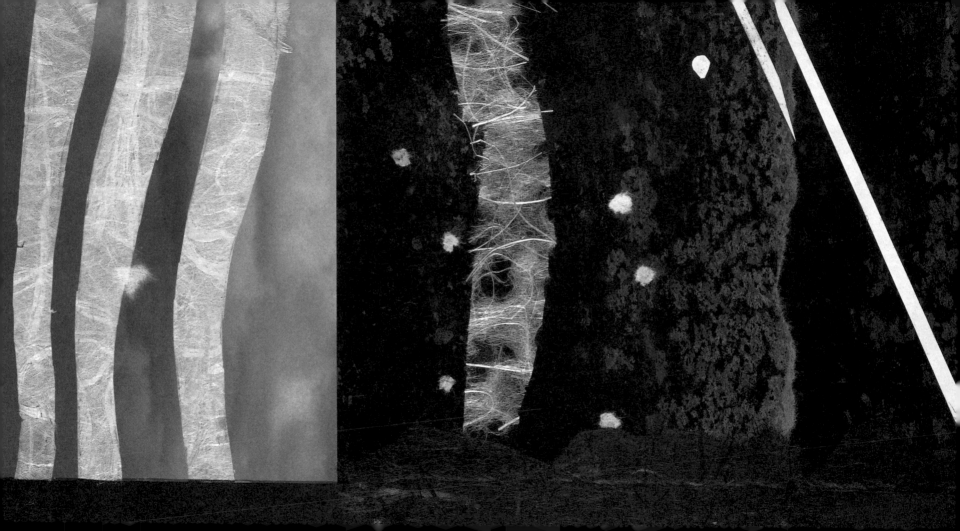

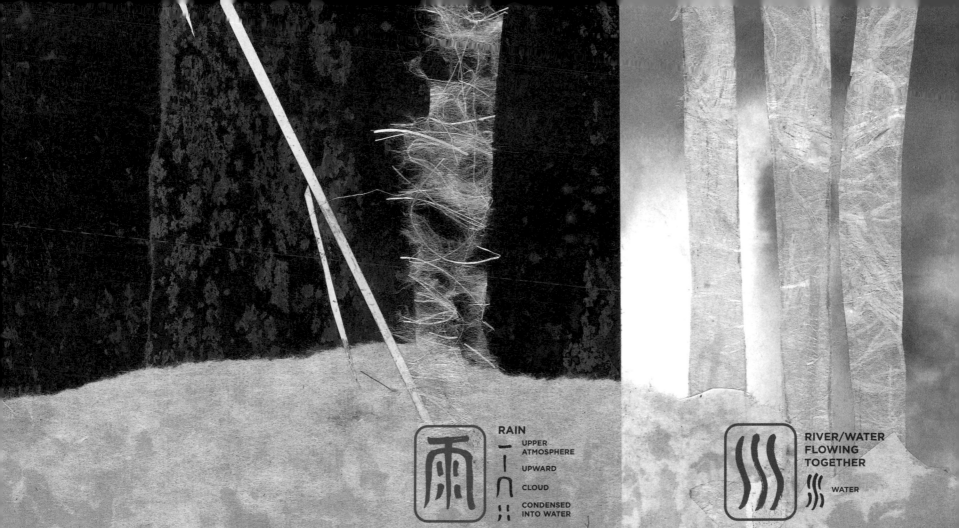

RAIN
— — — UPPER ATMOSPHERE
— 丨 — UPWARD
CLOUD
CONDENSED INTO WATER

RIVER/WATER FLOWING TOGETHER
WATER

IN ITS SKY, MIST ROSE AND FELL, RAIN WATER GATHERING, RIVER CASCADING

BOULDER

CLIFF

ROCK

THROUGH

DOWN CLIFFS AND BOULDERS, THROUGH VALLEYS INTO FIELDS.

SUN   MOON

As SUN, MOON KEPT WATCH, EARTH GAVE BIRTH

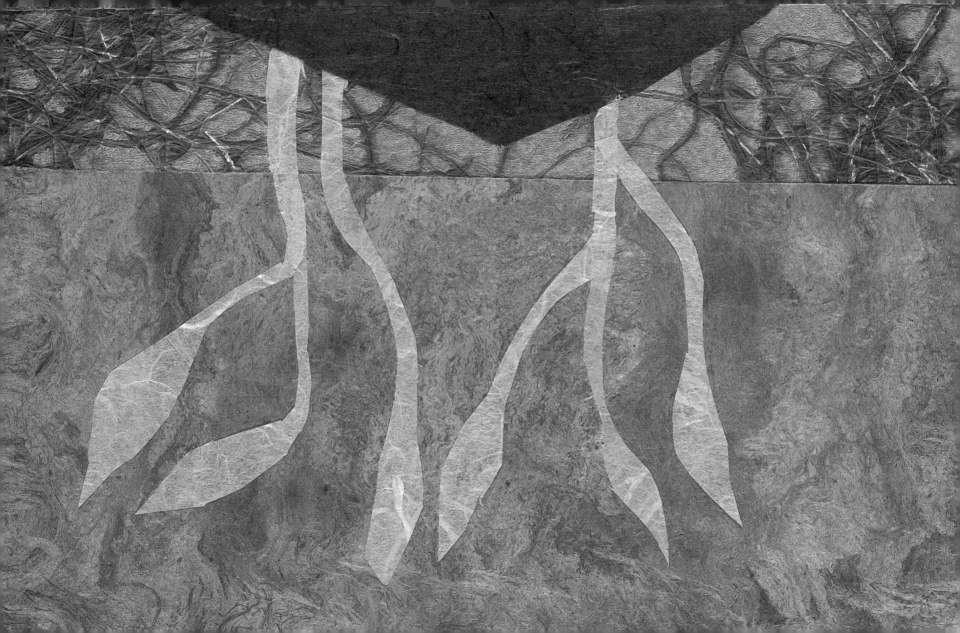

MANY
PLANTS

METAL
△ CLIFF
土 EARTH
八 NUGGETS

TO SPROUTS ABOVE, METAL BELOW,

TREE OF HANGING
TASSLE GRAIN

TREE

HANGING TASSLE

RICE

TREES OF HANGING GRAINS, CORN, WHEAT, MILLET AND RICE.

ICE

FIRE

IN WINTER'S ICE, SUMMER'S FIRE, MORE PLANTS FLOURISHED.

BAMBOO/
HANGING
LEAVES

LEEK

One of Drooping Leaves, Bamboo; of Even-Rowed, Leek;

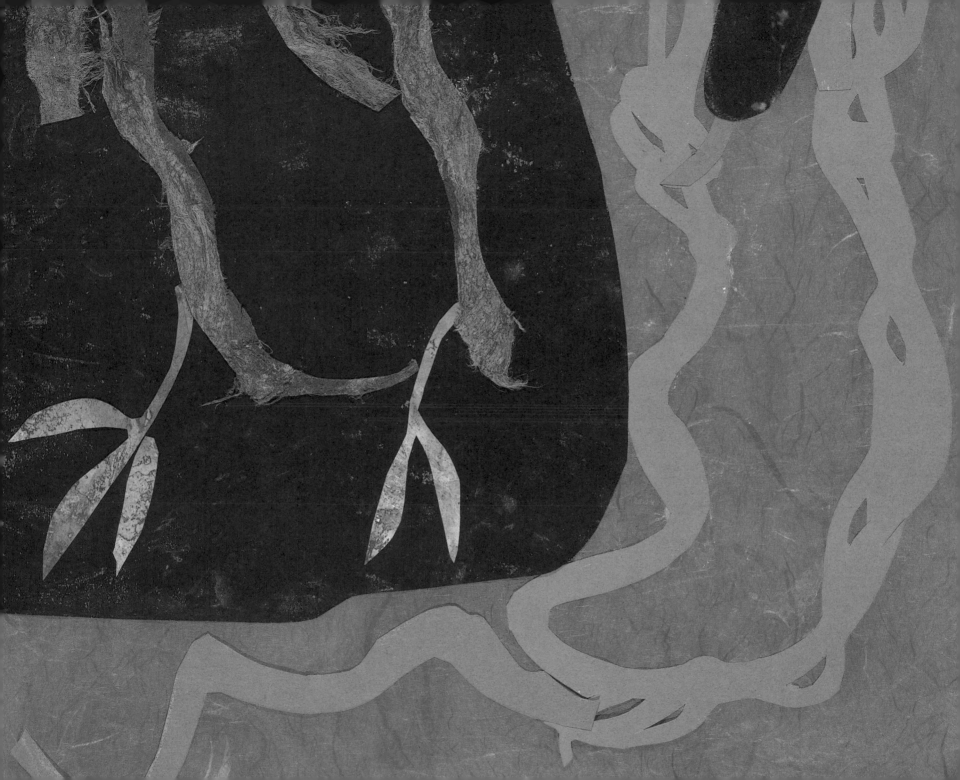

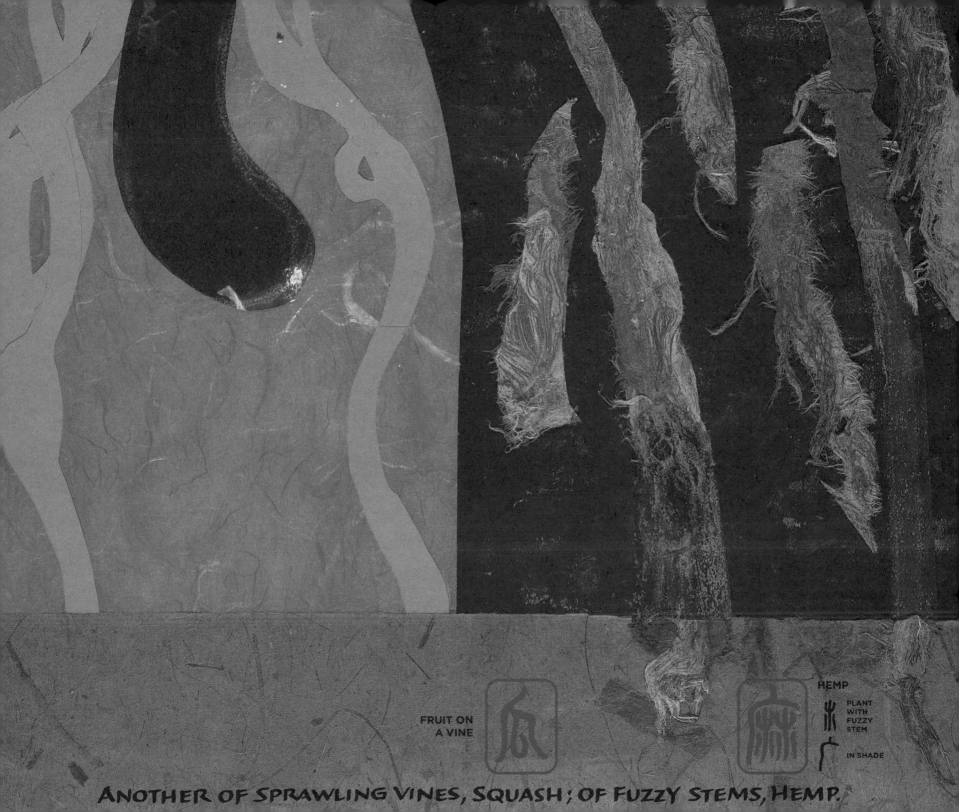

FRUIT ON
A VINE

HEMP

PLANT
WITH
FUZZY
STEM

IN SHADE

ANOTHER OF SPRAWLING VINES, SQUASH; OF FUZZY STEMS, HEMP.

WEST

BIRD

ROOST

SALT

GRAINS

TO THE WEST, WHERE BIRDS ROOST, A ROCK OF WONDER, SALT, WAS FOUND.

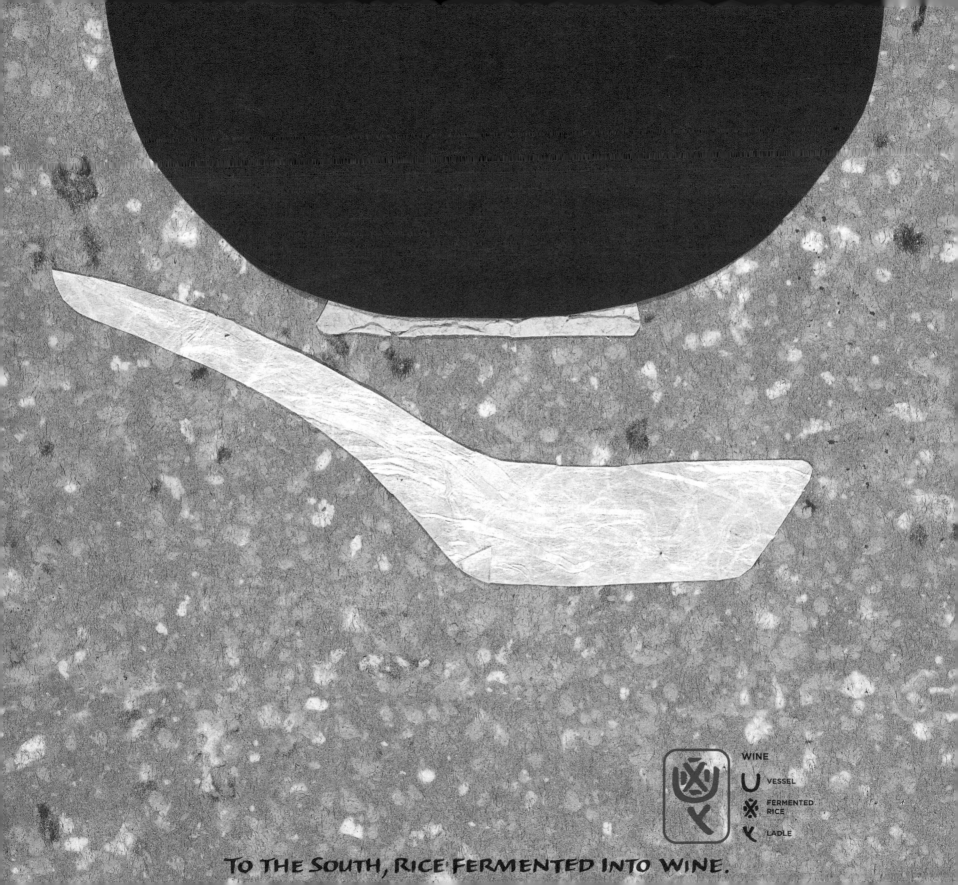

WINE

VESSEL

FERMENTED
RICE

LADLE

TO THE SOUTH, RICE FERMENTED INTO WINE.

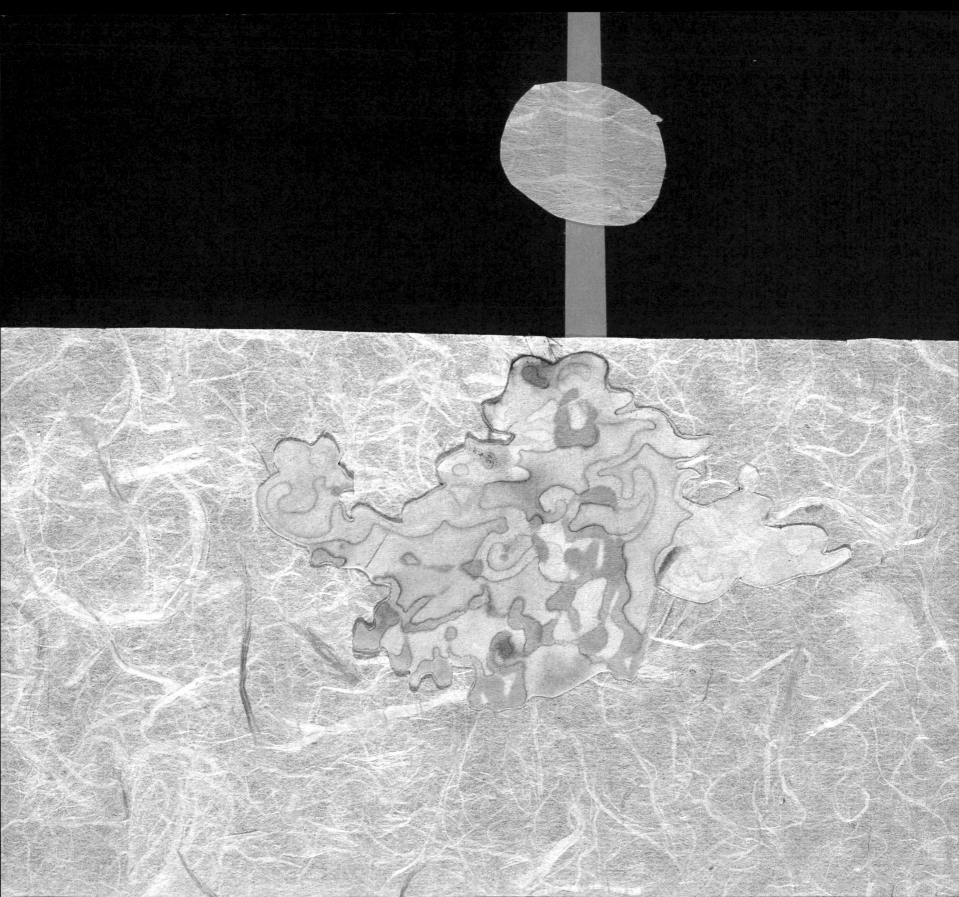

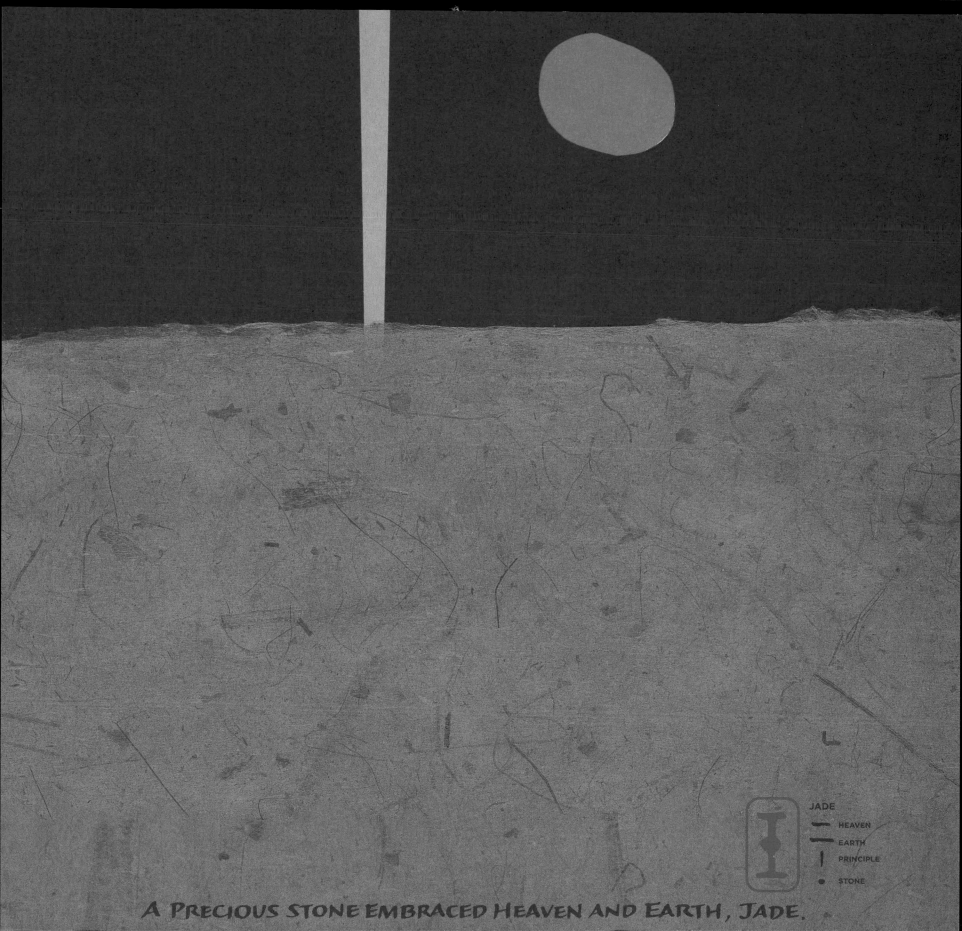

A Precious Stone Embraced Heaven and Earth, Jade.

JADE
— HEAVEN
— EARTH
! PRINCIPLE
• STONE

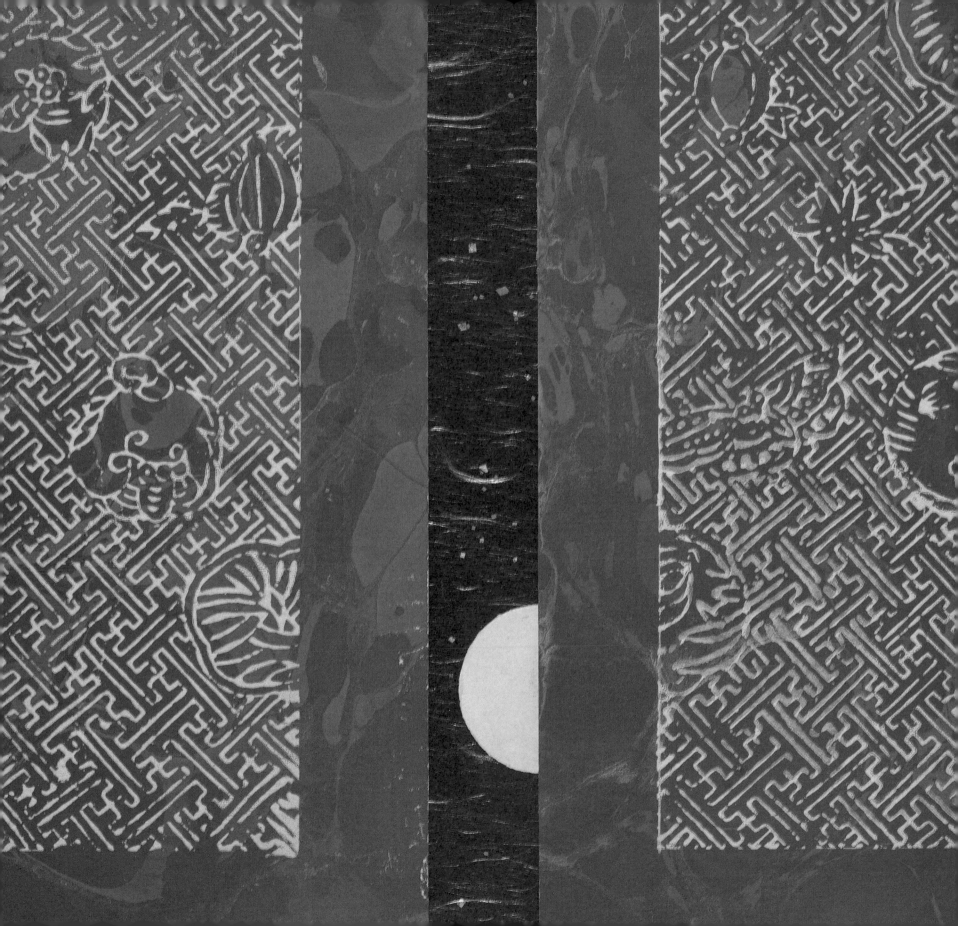

CENTER/MIDDLE

 TARGET

ARROW

KINGDOM

BOUNDARY

JADE (ON
KING'S CROWN)

THIS WAS MIDDLE EMPIRE, CHINA.

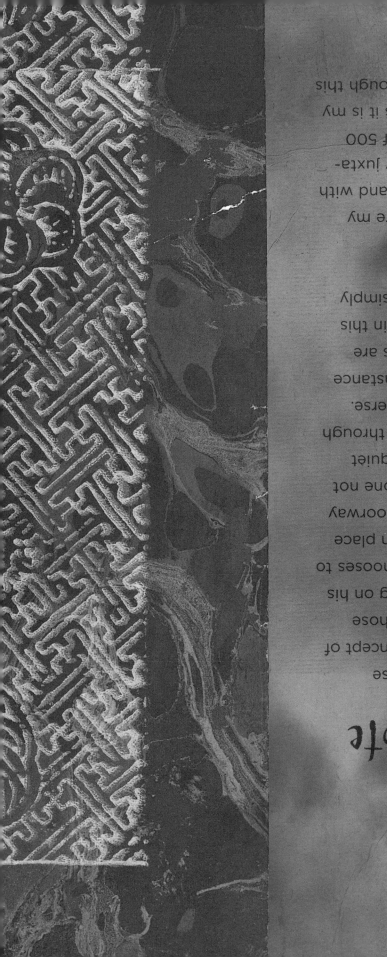

Author's Note

Once, I asked a Western artist to use Western symbols to describe his concept of the word *leisure*. He immediately chose to describe it with a person floating on his back in water. The Chinese mind chooses to be less literal—for instance, one can place a moon between two panels of a doorway to show a state of mind by which one not only notices, but also admires the quiet beauty of a moonbeam peeking in through that sliver. I think of this as visual verse. Rather than showing a particular instance of the idea, it reminds us that ideas are bigger than a single instance. And in this case reminds us that leisure is not simply an activity but a state of being.

The purpose of this book is to share my fascination with this poetic notion and with the hidden wisdom of symbols. By juxta-posing the seal-style characters (of 500 B.C.) against more modern symbols it is my hope that my readers will peek through this doorway and be open as well.

Be open to inspiration.
Inspiration leads to creativity.

Be open to play.
In play we see mistakes
as stepping-stones to fulfillment.

Be open to challenges.
Challenges offer us a chance to grow.

Be open to work.
It is in the willingness to labor
that we mature
and find excellence.

To my little Jewish sister,
Jeanette Lauritson,
who shared childhood with me

Chinese Characters Then and Now

Written language changes over time based on the needs of the people who use it. The Chinese characters used throughout this book are approximately 2,500 years old. Here is a chart that compares how they look compared to more modern versions:

	ANCIENT CHARACTER circa 500 B.C.	MODERN CHARACTER 20th century		ANCIENT CHARACTER circa 500 B.C.	MODERN CHARACTER 20th century
mountain peaks		山	hanging grain		禾
tree		木	ice		冰
east		東	bamboo/ hanging leaves		竹
water		水	leek		韭
rain		雨	fruit on a vine		瓜
river		川	hemp		麻
boulder		石	west		卤